TABLE OF CONTENTS

FOREWORD

Publication of the United States Government Interagency Domestic Terrorism Concept of Operations Plan (CONPLAN) represents a concerted effort by a number of Federal departments and agencies to work together to achieve a common goal. The CONPLAN was developed through the efforts of six primary departments and agencies with responsibilities as identified in Presidential Decision Directive/NSC-39 (PDD-39). This plan has been developed consistent with relevant PDDs, Federal law, the Attorney General's Critical Incident Response Plan, the PDD-39 Domestic Guidelines, and the Federal Response Plan and its Terrorism Incident Annex. The FBI has worked with these departments and agencies to provide a forum to participate in planning and exercise activities in order to develop, maintain, and enhance the Federal response capability.

To ensure the policy in PDD-39 and PDD-62 is implemented in a coordinated manner, the CONPLAN is designed to provide overall guidance to Federal, State and local agencies concerning how the Federal government would respond to a potential or actual terrorist threat or incident that occurs in the United States, particularly one involving Weapons of Mass Destruction (WMD). The CONPLAN outlines an organized and unified capability for a timely, coordinated response by Federal agencies to a terrorist threat or act. It establishes conceptual guidance for assessing and monitoring a developing threat, notifying appropriate Federal, State, and local agencies of the nature of the threat, and deploying the requisite advisory and technical resources to assist the Lead Federal Agency (LFA) in facilitating interdepartmental coordination of crisis and consequence management activities.

Actions will continue to refine and identify the mission, capabilities, and resources of other supporting departments and agencies; and the actions each agency or department must perform during each phase of the response, to include crisis management and consequence management actions that are necessary for chemical, biological, nuclear/radiological, and conventional materials or devices.

Inquiries concerning this CONPLAN should be addressed to the appropriate Lead Agency under this plan:

- Federal Bureau of Investigation, Counterterrorism Division, Domestic Terrorism/Counterterrorism Planning Section, for Crisis Management, or

- Federal Emergency Management Agency, Response and Recovery Directorate, Operations and Planning Division, for Consequence Management.

LETTER OF AGREEMENT

The United States Government Interagency Domestic Terrorism Concept of Operations Plan, hereafter referred to as the CONPLAN, is designed to provide overall guidance to Federal, State and local agencies concerning how the Federal government would respond to a potential or actual terrorist threat or incident that occurs in the United States, particularly one involving WMD.

The following departments and agencies agree to support the overall concept of operations of the CONPLAN in order to carry out their assigned responsibilities under PDD-39 and PDD-62. The departments and agencies also agree to implement national and regional planning efforts and exercise activities in order to maintain the overall Federal response capability. Specifically:

- The Attorney General is responsible for ensuring the development and implementation of policies directed at preventing terrorist attacks domestically, and will undertake the criminal prosecution of these acts of terrorism that violate U.S. law. The Department of Justice has charged the Federal Bureau of Investigation with execution of its LFA responsibilities for the management of a Federal response to terrorist incidents. As the lead agency for crisis management, the FBI will implement a Federal crisis management response. As LFA, the FBI will designate a Federal on-scene commander (OSC) to ensure appropriate coordination of the overall United States Government response with Federal, State and local authorities until such time as the Attorney General transfers the LFA role to the Federal Emergency Management Agency (FEMA).

- As the lead agency for consequence management, FEMA will implement the Federal Response Plan (FRP) to manage and coordinate the Federal consequence management response in support of State and local authorities.

- The Department of Defense will provide military assistance to the LFA and/or the CONPLAN primary agencies during all aspects of a terrorist incident upon request by the appropriate authority and approval by the Secretary of Defense.

- The Department of Energy will provide scientific-technical personnel and equipment in support of the LFA during all aspects of a nuclear/radiological WMD terrorist incident.

- The Environmental Protection Agency will provide technical personnel and supporting equipment to the LFA during all aspects of a WMD terrorist incident.

- The Department of Health and Human Services is the primary agency to plan and to prepare for a national response to medical emergencies arising from the terrorist use of WMD. HHS provides technical personnel and supporting equipment to the LFA during all aspects of a terrorist incident.

SIGNATORIES TO THE UNITED STATES GOVERNMENT INTERAGENCY DOMESTIC TERRORISM CONCEPT OF OPERATIONS PLAN

Secretary
Department of Defense

Secretary
Department of Energy

Secretary
Department of Health and Human Services

Administrator
Environmental Protection Agency

Director
Federal Emergency Management Agency

Director
Federal Bureau of Investigation

Attorney General
Department of Justice

I. INTRODUCTION AND BACKGROUND

A. Introduction

The ability of the United States Government to prevent, deter, defeat and respond decisively to terrorist attacks against our citizens, whether these attacks occur domestically, in international waters or airspace, or on foreign soil, is one of the most challenging priorities facing our nation today. The United States regards all such terrorism as a potential threat to national security, as well as a violent criminal act, and will apply all appropriate means to combat this danger. In doing so, the United States vigorously pursues efforts to deter and preempt these crimes and to apprehend and prosecute directly, or assist other governments in prosecuting, individuals who perpetrate or plan such terrorist attacks.

In 1995, President Clinton signed Presidential Decision Directive 39 (PDD-39), the United States Policy on Counterterrorism. This Presidential Directive built upon previous directives for combating terrorism and further elaborated a strategy and an interagency coordination mechanism and management structure to be undertaken by the Federal government to combat both domestic and international terrorism in all its forms. This authority includes implementing measures to reduce our vulnerabilities, deterring terrorism through a clear public position, responding rapidly and effectively to threats or actual terrorist acts, and giving the highest priority to developing sufficient capabilities to combat and manage the consequences of terrorist incidents involving weapons of mass destruction (WMD).

To ensure this policy is implemented in a coordinated manner, the Concept of Operations Plan, hereafter referred to as the CONPLAN, is designed to provide overall guidance to Federal, State and local agencies concerning how the Federal government would respond to a potential or actual terrorist threat or incident that occurs in the United States, particularly one involving WMD. The CONPLAN outlines an organized and unified capability for a timely, coordinated response by Federal agencies to a terrorist threat or act. It establishes conceptual guidance for assessing and monitoring a developing threat, notifying appropriate Federal, State, and local agencies of the nature of the threat, and deploying the requisite advisory and technical resources to assist the Lead Federal Agency (LFA) in facilitating interagency/interdepartmental coordination of a crisis and consequence management response. Lastly, it defines the relationships between structures under which the Federal government will marshal crisis and consequence management resources to respond to a threatened or actual terrorist incident.

B. Purpose

The purpose of this plan is to facilitate an effective Federal response to all threats or acts of terrorism within the United States that are determined to be of sufficient magnitude to warrant implementation of this plan and the associated policy guidelines established in PDD-39 and PDD-62. To accomplish this, the CONPLAN:

- Establishes a structure for a systematic, coordinated and effective national response to threats or acts of terrorism in the United States;

- Defines procedures for the use of Federal resources to augment and support local and State governments; and

- Encompasses both crisis and consequence management responsibilities, and articulates the coordination relationships between these missions.

C. Scope

The CONPLAN is a strategic document that:

- Applies to all threats or acts of terrorism within the United States;

- Provides planning guidance and outlines operational concepts for the Federal crisis and consequence management response to a threatened or actual terrorist incident within the United States;

- Serves as the foundation for further development of detailed national, regional, State, and local operations plans and procedures;

- Includes guidelines for notification, coordination and leadership of response activities, supporting operations, and coordination of emergency public information across all levels of government;

- Acknowledges the unique nature of each incident, the capabilities of the local jurisdiction, and the activities necessary to prevent or mitigate a specific threat or incident; and

- Illustrates ways in which Federal, State and local agencies can most effectively unify and synchronize their response actions.

D. Primary Federal Agencies

The response to a terrorist threat or incident within the U.S. will entail a highly coordinated, multi-agency local, State, and Federal response. In support of this mission, the following primary Federal agencies will provide the core Federal response:

- Department of Justice (DOJ) / Federal Bureau of Investigation (FBI) *
- Federal Emergency Management Agency (FEMA) **
- Department of Defense (DOD)
- Department of Energy (DOE)
- Environmental Protection Agency (EPA)
- Department of Health and Human Services (DHHS)

> * Lead Agency for Crisis Management
> ** Lead Agency for Consequence Management

Although not formally designated under the CONPLAN, other Federal departments and agencies may have authorities, resources, capabilities, or expertise required to support response operations. Agencies may be requested to participate in Federal planning and response operations, and may be asked to designate staff to function as liaison officers and provide other support to the LFA.

E. Primary Agency Responsibilities

1. Department of Justice (DOJ)/ Federal Bureau of Investigation (FBI)

The Attorney General is responsible for ensuring the development and implementation of policies directed at preventing terrorist attacks domestically, and will undertake the criminal prosecution of these acts of terrorism that violate U.S. law. DOJ has charged the FBI with execution of its LFA responsibilities for the management of a Federal response to terrorist threats or incidents that take place within U.S. territory or those occurring in international waters that do not involve the flag vessel of a foreign country. As the lead agency for crisis management, the FBI will implement a Federal crisis management response. As LFA, the FBI will designate a Federal on-scene commander to ensure appropriate coordination of the overall United States Government response with Federal, State and local authorities until such time as the Attorney General transfers the overall LFA role to FEMA. The FBI, with appropriate approval, will form and coordinate the deployment of a Domestic Emergency Support Team (DEST) with other agencies, when appropriate, and seek appropriate Federal support based on the nature of the situation.

2. Federal Emergency Management Agency (FEMA)

As the lead agency for consequence management, FEMA will manage and coordinate any Federal consequence management response in support of State and local governments in accordance with its statutory authorities. Additionally, FEMA will designate appropriate liaison and advisory personnel for the FBI's Strategic Information and Operations Center (SIOC) and deployment with the DEST, the Joint Operations Center (JOC), and the Joint Information Center (JIC).

3. Department of Defense (DOD)

DOD serves as a support agency to the FBI for crisis management functions, including technical operations, and a support agency to FEMA for consequence management. In accordance with DOD Directives 3025.15 and 2000.12 and the Chairman Joint Chiefs of Staff CONPLAN 0300-97, and upon approval by the Secretary of Defense, DOD will provide assistance to the LFA and/or the CONPLAN primary agencies, as appropriate, during all aspects of a terrorist incident, including both crisis and consequence management. DOD assistance includes threat assessment; DEST participation and transportation; technical advice; operational support; tactical support; support for civil disturbances; custody, transportation and disposal of a WMD device; and other capabilities including mitigation of the consequences of a release.

DOD has many unique capabilities for dealing with a WMD and combating terrorism, such as the US Army Medical Research Institute for Infectious Diseases, Technical Escort Unit, and US Marine Corps Chemical Biological Incident Response Force. These and other DOD assets may be used in responding to a terrorist incident if requested by the LFA and approved by the Secretary of Defense.

4. Department of Energy (DOE)

DOE serves as a support agency to the FBI for technical operations and a support agency to FEMA for consequence management. DOE provides scientific-technical personnel and equipment in support of the LFA during all aspects of a nuclear/radiological WMD terrorist incident. DOE assistance can support both crisis and consequence management activities with capabilities such as threat assessment, DEST deployment, LFA advisory requirements, technical advice, forecasted modeling predictions, and operational support to include direct support of tactical operations. Deployable DOE scientific technical assistance and support includes capabilities such as search operations; access operations; diagnostic and device assessment; radiological assessment and monitoring;

identification of material; development of Federal protective action recommendations; provision of information on the radiological response; render safe operations; hazards assessment; containment, relocation and storage of special nuclear material evidence; post-incident clean-up; and on-site management and radiological assessment to the public, the White House, and members of Congress and foreign governments. All DOE support to a Federal response will be coordinated through a Senior Energy Official.

5.   Environmental Protection Agency (EPA)

EPA serves as a support agency to the FBI for technical operations and a support agency to FEMA for consequence management. EPA provides technical personnel and supporting equipment to the LFA during all aspects of a WMD terrorist incident. EPA assistance may include threat assessment, DEST and regional emergency response team deployment, LFA advisory requirements, technical advice and operational support for chemical, biological, and radiological releases. EPA assistance and advice includes threat assessment, consultation, agent identification, hazard detection and reduction, environmental monitoring; sample and forensic evidence collection/analysis; identification of contaminants; feasibility assessment and clean-up; and on-site safety, protection, prevention, decontamination, and restoration activities. EPA and the United States Coast Guard (USCG) share responsibilities for response to oil discharges into navigable waters and releases of hazardous substances, pollutants, and contaminants into the environment under the National Oil and Hazardous Substances Pollution Contingency Plan (NCP). EPA provides the predesignated Federal On-Scene Coordinator for inland areas and the USCG for coastal areas to coordinate containment, removal, and disposal efforts and resources during an oil, hazardous substance, or WMD incident.

6.   Department of Health and Human Services (HHS)

HHS serves as a support agency to the FBI for technical operations and a support agency to FEMA for consequence management. HHS provides technical personnel and supporting equipment to the LFA during all aspects of a terrorist incident. HHS can also provide regulatory follow-up when an incident involves a product regulated by the Food and Drug Administration. HHS assistance supports threat assessment, DEST deployment, epidemiological investigation, LFA advisory requirements, and technical advice. Technical assistance to the FBI may include identification of agents, sample collection and analysis, on-site safety and protection activities, and medical management planning. Operational support to FEMA may include mass immunization, mass prophylaxis, mass fatality management, pharmaceutical support operations (National Pharmaceutical Stockpile), contingency medical records, patient tracking, and patient evacuation and definitive medical care provided through the National Disaster Medical System.

II. POLICIES

A. Authorities

The following authorities are the basis for the development of the CONPLAN:

- Presidential Decision Directive 39, including the Domestic Guidelines
- Presidential Decision Directive 62
- Robert T. Stafford Disaster Relief and Emergency Assistance Act

B. Other Plans and Directives

- Federal Response Plan, including the Terrorism Incident Annex
- Federal Radiological Emergency Response Plan
- National Oil and Hazardous Substances Pollution Contingency Plan
- HHS Health and Medical Services Support Plan for the Federal Response to Assets of Chemical/Biological Terrorism
- Chairman of the Joint Chiefs of Staff CONPLAN 0300/0400
- DODD 3025.15 Military Assistance to Civil Authorities
- Other Department of Defense Directives

C. Federal Agency Authorities

The CONPLAN does not supersede existing plans or authorities that were developed for response to incidents under department and agency statutory authorities. Rather, it is intended to be a coordinating plan between crisis and consequence management to provide an effective Federal response to terrorism. The CONPLAN is a Federal signatory plan among the six principal departments and agencies named in PDD-39. It may be updated and amended, as necessary, by consensus among these agencies.

D.   Federal Response to a Terrorism Incident

The Federal response to a terrorist threat or incident provides a tailored, time-phased deployment of specialized Federal assets. The response is executed under two broad responsibilities:

1.   Crisis Management

Crisis management is predominantly a law enforcement function and includes measures to identify, acquire, and plan the use of resources needed to anticipate, prevent, and/or resolve a threat or act of terrorism. In a terrorist incident, a crisis management response may include traditional law enforcement missions, such as intelligence, surveillance, tactical operations, negotiations, forensics, and investigations, as well as technical support missions, such as agent identification, search, render safe procedures, transfer and disposal, and limited decontamination. In addition to the traditional law enforcement missions, crisis management also includes assurance of public health and safety.

The laws of the United States assign primary authority to the Federal government to prevent and respond to acts of terrorism or potential acts of terrorism. Based on the situation, a Federal crisis management response may be supported by technical operations, and by consequence management activities, which should operate concurrently.

2.   Consequence Management

Consequence management is predominantly an emergency management function and includes measures to protect public health and safety, restore essential government services, and provide emergency relief to governments, businesses, and individuals affected by the consequences of terrorism. In an actual or potential terrorist incident, a consequence management response will be managed by FEMA using structures and resources of the Federal Response Plan (FRP). These efforts will include support missions as described in other Federal operations plans, such as predictive modeling, protective action recommendations, and mass decontamination.

The laws of the United States assign primary authority to the State and local governments to respond to the consequences of terrorism; the Federal government provides assistance, as required.

E. Lead Federal Agency Designation

As mandated by the authorities referenced above, the operational response to a terrorist threat will employ a coordinated, interagency process organized through a LFA concept. PDD-39 reaffirms and elaborates on the U.S. Government's policy on counterterrorism and expands the roles, responsibilities and management structure for combating terrorism. LFA responsibility is assigned to the Department of Justice, and is delegated to the FBI, for threats or acts of terrorism that take place in the United States or in international waters that do not involve the flag vessel of a foreign country. Within this role, the FBI Federal on-scene commander (OSC) will function as the on-scene manager for the U.S. Government. All Federal agencies and departments, as needed, will support the Federal OSC. Threats or acts of terrorism that take place outside of the United States or its trust territories, or in international waters and involve the flag vessel of a foreign country are outside the scope of the CONPLAN.

In addition, these authorities reaffirm that FEMA is the lead agency for consequence management within U.S. territory. FEMA retains authority and responsibility to act as the lead agency for consequence management throughout the Federal response. FEMA will use the FRP structure to coordinate all Federal assistance to State and local governments for consequence management. To ensure that there is one overall LFA, PDD-39 directs FEMA to support the Department of Justice (as delegated to the FBI) until the Attorney General transfers the LFA role to FEMA. At such time, the responsibility to function as the on-scene manager for the U.S. Government transfers from the FBI Federal OSC to the Federal Coordinating Officer (FCO).

F. Requests For Federal Assistance

Requests for Federal assistance by State and local governments, as well as those from owners and operators of critical infrastructure facilities, are coordinated with the lead agency (crisis or consequence) responsible under U.S. law for that function. In response to a terrorist threat or incident, multiple or competing requests will be managed based on priorities and objectives established by the JOC Command Group.

State and local governments will submit requests for Federal crisis management assistance through the FBI. State and local governments will submit requests for Federal consequence management assistance through standard channels under the Federal Response Plan. FEMA liaisons assigned to the DEST or JOC coordinate requests with the LFA to ensure consequence management plans and actions are consistent with overall priorities. All other requests for consequence management assistance submitted outside normal channels to the DEST or JOC will be forwarded to the Regional Operations Center (ROC) Director or the Federal Coordinating Officer (FCO) for action.

G.   Funding

As mandated by PDD-39, Federal agencies directed to participate in counterterrorist operations or the resolution of terrorist incidents bear the costs of their own participation, unless otherwise directed by the President. This responsibility is subject to specific statutory authorization to provide support without reimbursement. In the absence of such specific authority, the Economy Act applies, and reimbursement cannot be waived.

H.   Deployment/Employment Priorities

The multi-agency JOC Command Group, managed by the Federal OSC, ensures that conflicts are resolved, overall incident objectives are established, and strategies are selected for the use of critical resources. These strategies will be based on the following priorities:

1.   Preserving life or minimizing risk to health. This constitutes the first priority of operations.

2.   Preventing a threatened act from being carried out or an existing terrorist act from being expanded or aggravated.

3.   Locating, accessing, rendering safe, controlling, containing, recovering, and disposing of a WMD that has not yet functioned.

4.   Rescuing, decontaminating, transporting and treating victims. Preventing secondary casualties as a result of contamination or collateral threats.

5.   Releasing emergency public information that ensures adequate and accurate communications with the public from all involved response agencies.

6.   Restoring essential services and mitigating suffering.

7.   Apprehending and successfully prosecuting perpetrators.

8.   Conducting site restoration.

I.   Planning Assumptions and Considerations

1.   The CONPLAN assumes that no single private or government agency at the local, State, or Federal level possesses the authority and the expertise to act unilaterally on the difficult issues that may arise in

response to threats or acts of terrorism, particularly if nuclear, radiological, biological, or chemical materials are involved.

2. The CONPLAN is based on the premise that a terrorist incident may occur at any time of day with little or no warning, may involve single or multiple geographic areas, and result in mass casualties.

3. The CONPLAN also assumes an act of terrorism, particularly an act directed against a large population center within the United States involving nuclear, radiological, biological, or chemical materials, will have major consequences that can overwhelm the capabilities of many local and State governments to respond and may seriously challenge existing Federal response capabilities, as well.

4. Federal participating agencies may need to respond on short notice to provide effective and timely assistance to State and local governments.

5. Federal departments and agencies would be expected to provide an initial response when warranted under their own authorities and funding. Decisions to mobilize Federal assets will be coordinated with the FBI and FEMA.

6. In the case of a biological WMD attack, the effect may be temporally and geographically dispersed, with no determined or defined "incident site." Response operations may be conducted over a multi-jurisdictional, multi-State region.

7. A biological WMD attack employing a contagious agent may require quarantine by State and local health officials to contain the disease outbreak.

8. Local, State, and Federal responders will define working perimeters that overlap. Perimeters may be used by responders to control access to an affected area, to assign operational sectors among responding organizations, and to assess potential effects on the population and the environment. Control of these perimeters and response actions may be managed by different authorities, which will impede the effectiveness of the overall response if adequate coordination is not established.

9. If appropriate personal protective equipment and capabilities are not available and the area is contaminated with WMD materials, it is possible that response actions into a contaminated area may be delayed until the material has dissipated to a level that is safe for emergency response personnel to operate.

J.   Training and Exercises

Federal agencies, in conjunction with State and local governments, will periodically exercise their roles and responsibilities designated under the CONPLAN. Federal agencies should coordinate their exercises with the Exercise Subgroup of the Interagency Working Group on Counterterrorism and other response agencies to avoid duplication, and, more importantly, to provide a forum to exercise coordination mechanisms among responding agencies.

Federal agencies will assist State and local governments design and improve their response capabilities to a terrorist threat or incident. Each agency should coordinate its training programs with other response agencies to avoid duplication and to make its training available to other agencies.

III.   SITUATION

A.   Introduction

The complexity, scope, and potential consequences of a terrorist threat or incident require that there be a rapid and decisive capability to resolve the situation. The resolution to an act of terrorism demands an extraordinary level of coordination of crisis and consequence management functions and technical expertise across all levels of government. No single Federal, State, or local governmental agency has the capability or requisite authority to respond independently and mitigate the consequences of such a threat to national security. The incident may affect a single location or multiple locations, each of which may be a disaster scene, a hazardous scene and/or a crime scene simultaneously.

B.   Differences Between WMD Incidents and Other Incidents

As in all incidents, WMD incidents may involve mass casualties and damage to buildings or other types of property. However, there are several factors surrounding WMD incidents that are unlike any other type of incidents that must be taken into consideration when planning a response. First responders' ability to identify aspects of the incident (e.g., signs and symptoms exhibited by victims) and report them accurately will be key to maximizing the use of critical local resources and for triggering a Federal response.

    1.   The situation may not be recognizable until there are multiple casualties. Most chemical and biological agents are not detectable by methods used for explosives and firearms. Most agents can be carried in containers that look like ordinary items.

    2.   There may be multiple events (e.g., one event in an attempt to influence another event's outcome).

3.   Responders are placed at a higher risk of becoming casualties. Because agents are not readily identifiable, responders may become contaminated before recognizing the agent involved. First responders may, in addition, be targets for secondary releases or explosions.

4.   The location of the incident will be treated as a crime scene. As such, preservation and collection of evidence is critical. Therefore, it is important to ensure that actions on-scene are coordinated between response organizations to minimize any conflicts between law enforcement authorities, who view the incident as a crime scene, and other responders, who view it as a hazardous materials or disaster scene.

5.   Contamination of critical facilities and large geographic areas may result. Victims may carry an agent unknowingly to public transportation facilities, businesses, residences, doctors' offices, walk-in medical clinics, or emergency rooms because they don't realize that they are contaminated. First responders may carry the agent to fire or precinct houses, hospitals, or to the locations of subsequent calls.

6.   The scope of the incident may expand geometrically and may affect mutual aid jurisdictions. Airborne agents flow with the air current and may disseminate via ventilation systems, carrying the agents far from the initial source.

7.   There will be a stronger reaction from the public than with other types of incidents. The thought of exposure to a chemical or biological agent or radiation evokes terror in most people. The fear of the unknown also makes the public's response more severe.

8.   Time is working against responding elements. The incident can expand geometrically and very quickly. In addition, the effects of some chemicals and biological agents worsen over time.

9.   Support facilities, such as utility stations and 911 centers along with critical infrastructures, are at risk as targets.

10.   Specialized State and local response capabilities may be overwhelmed.

C.   Threat Levels

The CONPLAN establishes a range of threat levels determined by the FBI that serve to frame the nature and scope of the Federal response. Each threat level provides for an escalating range of actions that will be implemented concurrently for crisis and consequence management. The Federal government will take specific actions which are synchronized to each threat level, ensuring that all Federal agencies are operating with jointly and consistently executed plans. The Federal government will notify and coordinate with State and local governments, as necessary. The threat levels are described below:

1.   **Level #4 - Minimal Threat:**

Received threats do not warrant actions beyond normal liaison notifications or placing assets or resources on a heightened alert (agencies are operating under normal day-to-day conditions).

2.   **Level #3 - Potential Threat:**

Intelligence or an articulated threat indicates a potential for a terrorist incident. However, this threat has not yet been assessed as credible.

3.   **Level #2 - Credible Threat:**

A threat assessment indicates that the potential threat is credible, and confirms the involvement of WMD in the developing terrorist incident. Intelligence will vary with each threat, and will impact the level of the Federal response. At this threat level, the situation requires the tailoring of response actions to use Federal resources needed to anticipate, prevent, and/or resolve the crisis. The Federal crisis management response will focus on law enforcement actions taken in the interest of public safety and welfare, and is predominantly concerned with preventing and resolving the threat. The Federal consequence management response will focus on contingency planning and pre-positioning of tailored resources, as required. The threat increases in significance when the presence of an explosive device or WMD capable of causing a significant destructive event, prior to actual injury or loss, is confirmed or when intelligence and circumstances indicate a high probability that a device exists. In this case, the threat has developed into a WMD terrorist situation requiring an immediate process to identify, acquire, and plan the use of Federal resources to augment State and local authorities in lessening or averting the potential consequence of a terrorist use or employment of WMD.

4.   **Level #1 - WMD Incident:**

A WMD terrorism incident has occurred which requires an immediate process to identify, acquire, and plan the use of Federal resources to augment State and local authorities in response to limited or major consequences of a terrorist use or employment of WMD. This incident has resulted in mass casualties. The Federal response is primarily directed toward public safety and welfare and the preservation of human life.

D.   Lead Federal Agency Responsibilities

The LFA, in coordination with the appropriate Federal, State and local agencies, is responsible for formulating the Federal strategy and a coordinated Federal response. To accomplish that goal, the LFA must establish multi-agency coordination structures, as appropriate, at the incident scene, area, and national level. These structures are needed to perform oversight responsibilities in operations involving multiple agencies with direct statutory authority to respond to aspects of a single major incident or multiple incidents. Oversight responsibilities include:

- Coordination. Coordinate the determination of operational objectives, strategies, and priorities for the use of critical resources that have been allocated to the situation, and communicate multi-agency decisions back to individual agencies and incidents.

- Situation Assessment. Evaluate emerging threats, prioritize incidents, and project future needs.

- Public Information. As the spokesperson for the Federal response, the LFA is responsible for coordinating information dissemination to the White House, Congress, and other Federal, State and local government officials. In fulfilling this responsibility, the LFA ensures that the release of public information is coordinated between crisis and consequence management response entities. The Joint Information Center (JIC) is established by the LFA, under the operational control of the LFA's Public Information Officer, as a focal point for the coordination and provision of information to the public and media concerning the Federal response to the emergency. The JIC may be established in the same location as the FBI Joint Operations Center (JOC) or may be located at an on-scene location in coordination with State and local agencies. The following elements should be represented at the JIC: (1) FBI Public Information Officer and staff, (2) FEMA Public Information Officer and staff, (3) other Federal agency Public Information Officers, as needed, and (4) State and local Public Information Officers.

IV.   CONCEPT OF OPERATIONS

A.   Mission

The overall Lead Federal Agency, in conjunction with the lead agencies for crisis and consequence management response, and State and local authorities where appropriate, will notify, activate, deploy and employ Federal resources in response to a threat or act of terrorism. Operations will be conducted in accordance with statutory authorities and applicable plans and procedures, as modified by the policy guidelines established in PDD-39 and PDD-62. The overall LFA will continue operations until the crisis is resolved. Operations under the CONPLAN will then stand down, while operations under other Federal plans may continue to assist State and local governments with recovery.

B.   Command and Control

Command and control of a terrorist threat or incident is a critical function that demands a unified framework for the preparation and execution of plans and orders. Emergency response organizations at all levels of government may manage command and control activities somewhat differently depending on the organization's history, the complexity of the crisis, and their capabilities and resources. Management of Federal, State and local response actions must, therefore, reflect an inherent flexibility in order to effectively address the entire spectrum of capabilities and resources across the United States. The resulting challenge is to integrate the different types of management systems and approaches utilized by all levels of government into a comprehensive and unified response to meet the unique needs and requirements of each incident.

1.   Consequence Management

State and local consequence management organizations are generally structured to respond to an incident scene using a modular, functionally-oriented ICS that can be tailored to the kind, size and management needs of the incident. ICS is employed to organize and unify multiple disciplines with multi-jurisdictional responsibilities on-scene under one functional organization. State and local emergency operations plans generally establish direction and control procedures for their agencies' response to disaster situations. The organization's staff is built from a "top-down" approach with responsibility and authority placed initially with an Incident Commander who determines which local resources will be deployed. In many States, State law or local jurisdiction ordinances will identify by organizational position the person(s) that will be responsible for serving as the incident commander. In most cases, the incident commander will come from the State or local organization that has primary responsibility for managing the emergency situation.

When the magnitude of a crisis exceeds the capabilities and resources of the local incident commander or multiple jurisdictions become involved in order to resolve the crisis situation, the ICS command function can readily evolve into a Unified Command (see Figure 1). Under Unified Command, a multi-agency command post is established incorporating officials from agencies with jurisdictional responsibility at the incident scene. Multiple agency resources and personnel will then be integrated into the ICS as the single overall response management structure at the incident scene.

Multi-agency coordination to provide resources to support on-scene operations in complex or multiple incidents is the responsibility of emergency management. In the emergency management system, requests for resources are filled at the lowest possible level of government. Requests that exceed available capabilities are progressively forwarded until filled, from a local Emergency Operations Center (EOC), to a State EOC, to Federal operations centers at the regional or national level.

State assistance may be provided to local governments in responding to a terrorist threat or recovering from the consequences of a terrorist incident as in any natural or man-made disaster. The governor, by State law, is the chief executive officer of the State or commonwealth and has full authority to discharge the duties of his office and exercise all powers associated with the operational control of the State's emergency services during a declared emergency. State agencies are responsible for ensuring that essential services and resources are available to the local authorities and Incident Commander when requested. When State assistance is provided, the local government retains overall responsibility for command and control of the emergency operations, except in cases where State or Federal statutes transfer authority to a specific State or Federal agency. State and local governments have primary responsibility for consequence management. FEMA, using the FRP, directs and coordinates all Federal response efforts to manage the consequences in domestic incidents, for which the President has declared, or expressed an intent to declare, an emergency.

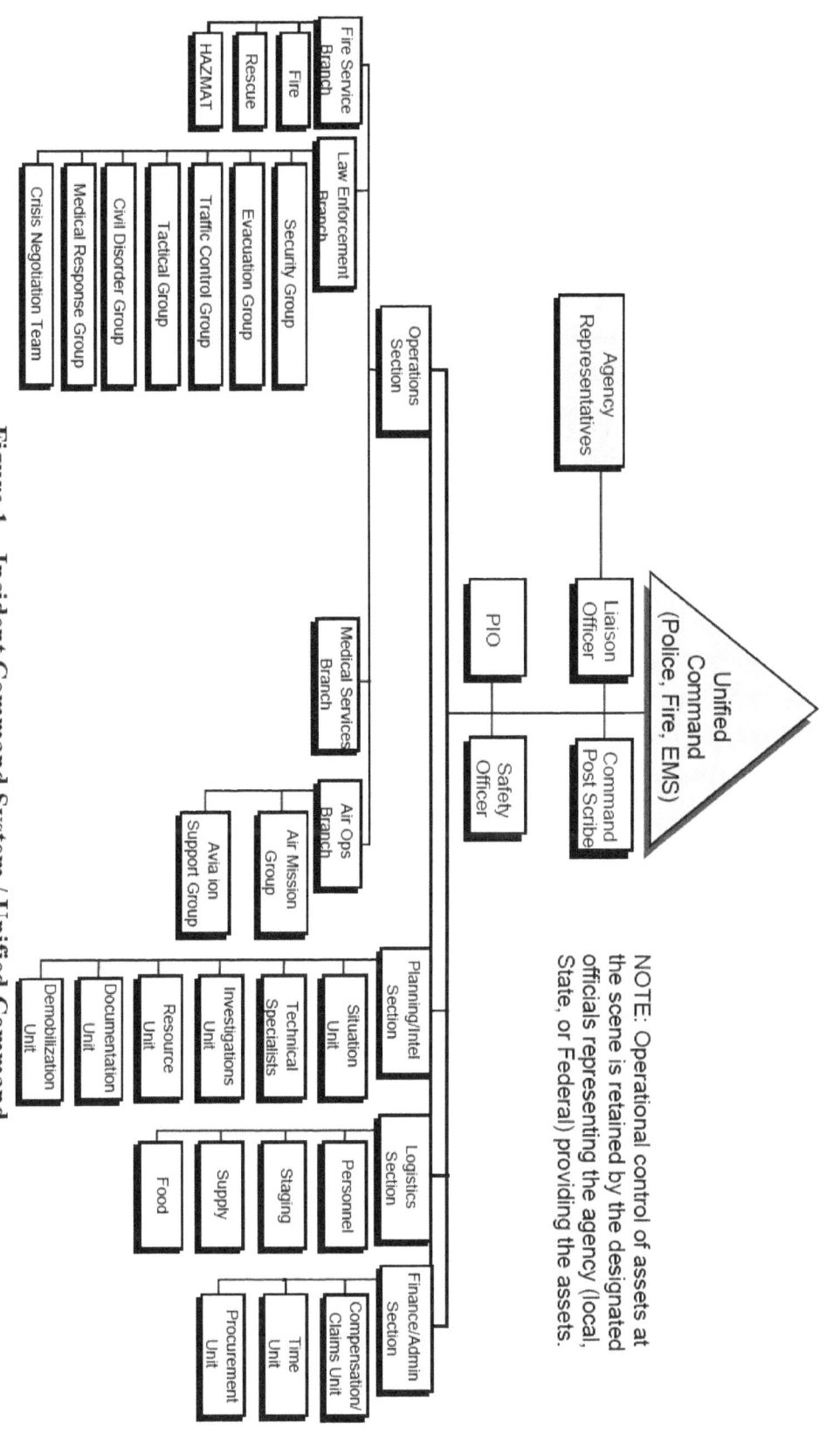

Figure 1 – Incident Command System / Unified Command

17

2. Crisis Management

As the lead agency for crisis management, the FBI manages a crisis situation from an FBI command post or JOC, bringing the necessary assets to respond and resolve the threat or incident. These activities primarily coordinate the law enforcement actions responding to the cause of the incident with State and local agencies.

During a crisis situation, the FBI Special Agent In Charge (SAC) of the local Field Division will establish a command post to manage the threat based upon a graduated and flexible response. This command post structure generally consists of three functional groups, Command, Operations, and Support, and is designed to accommodate participation of other agencies, as appropriate (see Figure 2). When the threat or incident exceeds the capabilities and resources of the local FBI Field Division, the SAC can request additional resources from the FBI's Critical Incident Response Group, located at Quantico, VA, to augment existing crisis management capabilities. In a terrorist threat or incident that may involve a WMD, the traditional FBI command post is expanded into a JOC incorporating a fourth functional entity, the Consequence Management Group.

Requests for DOD assistance for crisis management during the incident come from the Attorney General to the Secretary of Defense through the DOD Executive Secretary. Once the Secretary has approved the request, the order will be transmitted either directly to the unit involved or through the Chairman of the Joint Chiefs of Staff.

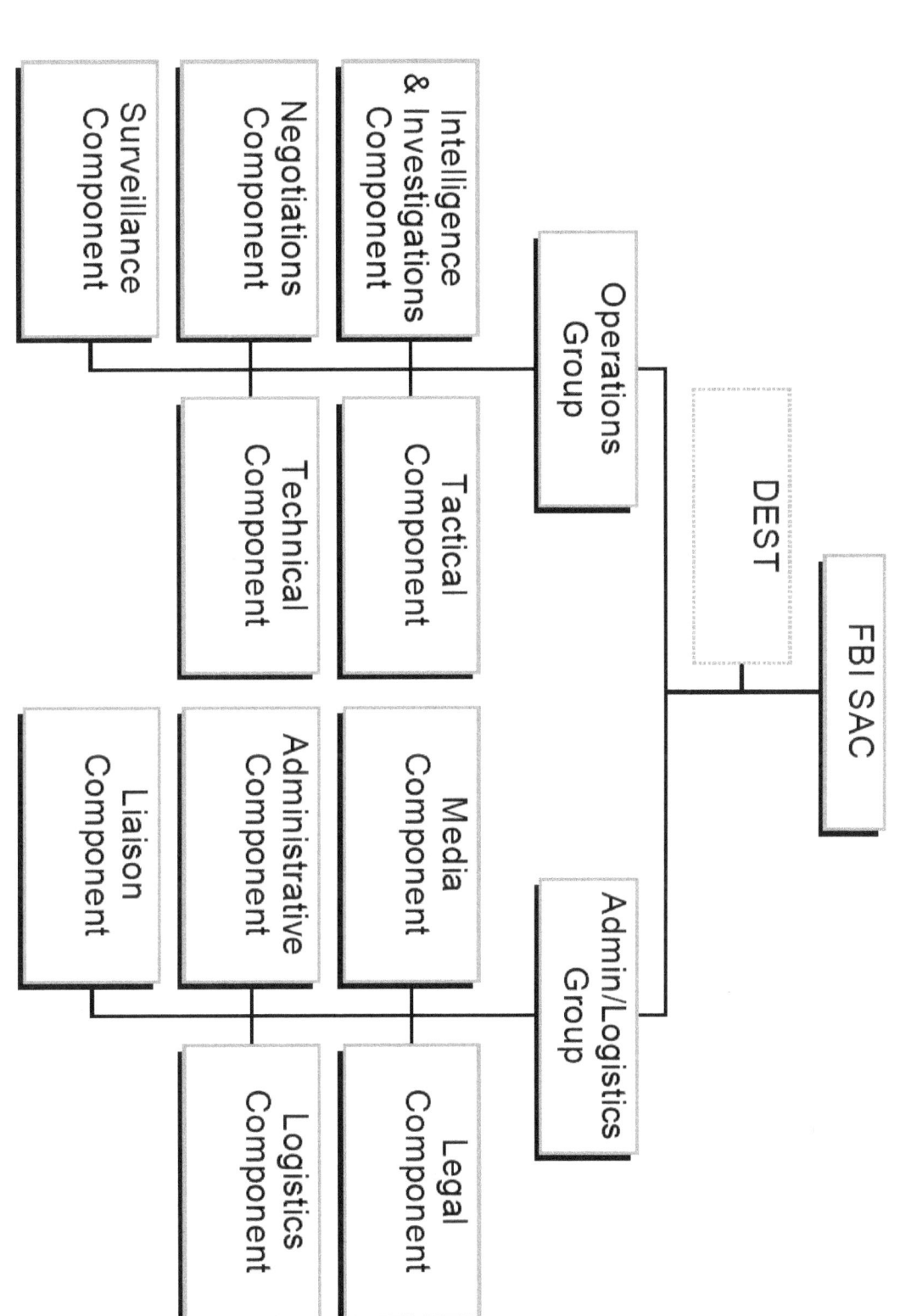

Figure 2 - FBI Command Post

19

C.   Unification of Federal, State and Local Response

1.   Introduction

Throughout the management of the terrorist incident, crisis and consequence management components will operate concurrently (see Figure 3). The concept of operations for a Federal response to a terrorist threat or incident provides for the designation of an LFA to ensure multi-agency coordination and a tailored, time-phased deployment of specialized Federal assets. It is critical that all participating Federal, State, and local agencies interact in a seamless manner.

2.   National Level Coordination

The complexity and potential catastrophic consequences of a terrorist event will require application of a multi-agency coordination system at the Federal agency headquarters level. Many critical on-scene decisions may need to be made in consultation with higher authorities. In addition, the transfer of information between the headquarters and field levels is critical to the successful resolution of the crisis incident.

Upon determination of a credible threat, FBI Headquarters (FBIHQ) will activate its Strategic Information and Operations Center (SIOC) to coordinate and manage the national level support to a terrorism incident. At this level, the SIOC will generally mirror the JOC structure operating in the field. The SIOC is staffed by liaison officers from other Federal agencies that are required to provide direct support to the FBI, in accordance with PDD-39. The SIOC performs the critical functions of coordinating the Federal response and facilitating Federal agency headquarters connectivity. Affected Federal agencies will operate headquarters-level emergency operations centers, as necessary.

Upon notification by the FBI of a credible terrorist threat, FEMA may activate its Catastrophic Disaster Response Group. In addition, FEMA will activate the Regional Operations Center and Emergency Support Team, as required.

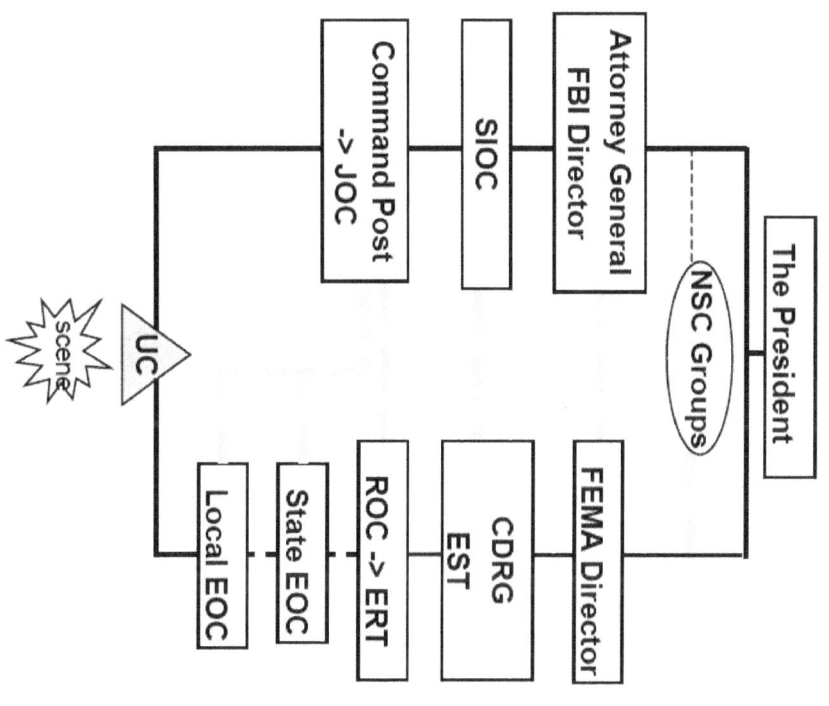

Figure 3 – Coordinating Relationships

21

3. Field Level Coordination

During a terrorist incident, the organizational structure to implement the Federal response at the field level is the JOC. The JOC is established by the FBI under the operational control of the Federal OSC, and acts as the focal point for the strategic management and direction of on-site activities, identification of State and local requirements and priorities, and coordination of the Federal response. The local FBI field office will activate a Crisis Management Team to establish the JOC, which will be in the affected area, possibly collocated with an existing emergency operations facility. Additionally, the JOC will be augmented by outside agencies, including representatives from the DEST (if deployed), who provide interagency technical expertise as well as inter-agency continuity during the transition from an FBI command post structure to the JOC structure.

Similar to the Area Command concept within the ICS, the JOC is established to ensure inter-incident coordination and to organize multiple agencies and jurisdictions within an overall command and coordination structure. The JOC includes the following functional groups: Command, Operations, Admin/Logistics, and Consequence Management (see Figure 4). Representation within the JOC includes officials from local, State and Federal agencies with specific roles in crisis and consequence management.

The Command Group of the JOC is responsible for providing recommendations and advice to the Federal OSC regarding the development and implementation of strategic decisions to resolve the crisis situation and for approving the deployment and employment of resources. In this scope, the members of the Command Group play an important role in ensuring the coordination of Federal crisis and consequence management functions. The Command Group is composed of the FBI Federal OSC and senior officials with decision making authority from local, State, and Federal agencies, as appropriate, based upon the circumstances of the threat or incident. Strategies, tactics and priorities are jointly determined within this group. While the FBI retains authority to make Federal crisis management decisions at all times, operational decisions are made cooperatively to the greatest extent possible. The FBI Federal OSC and the senior FEMA official at the JOC will provide, or obtain from higher authority, an immediate resolution of conflicts in priorities for allocation of critical Federal resources between the crisis and consequence management responses.

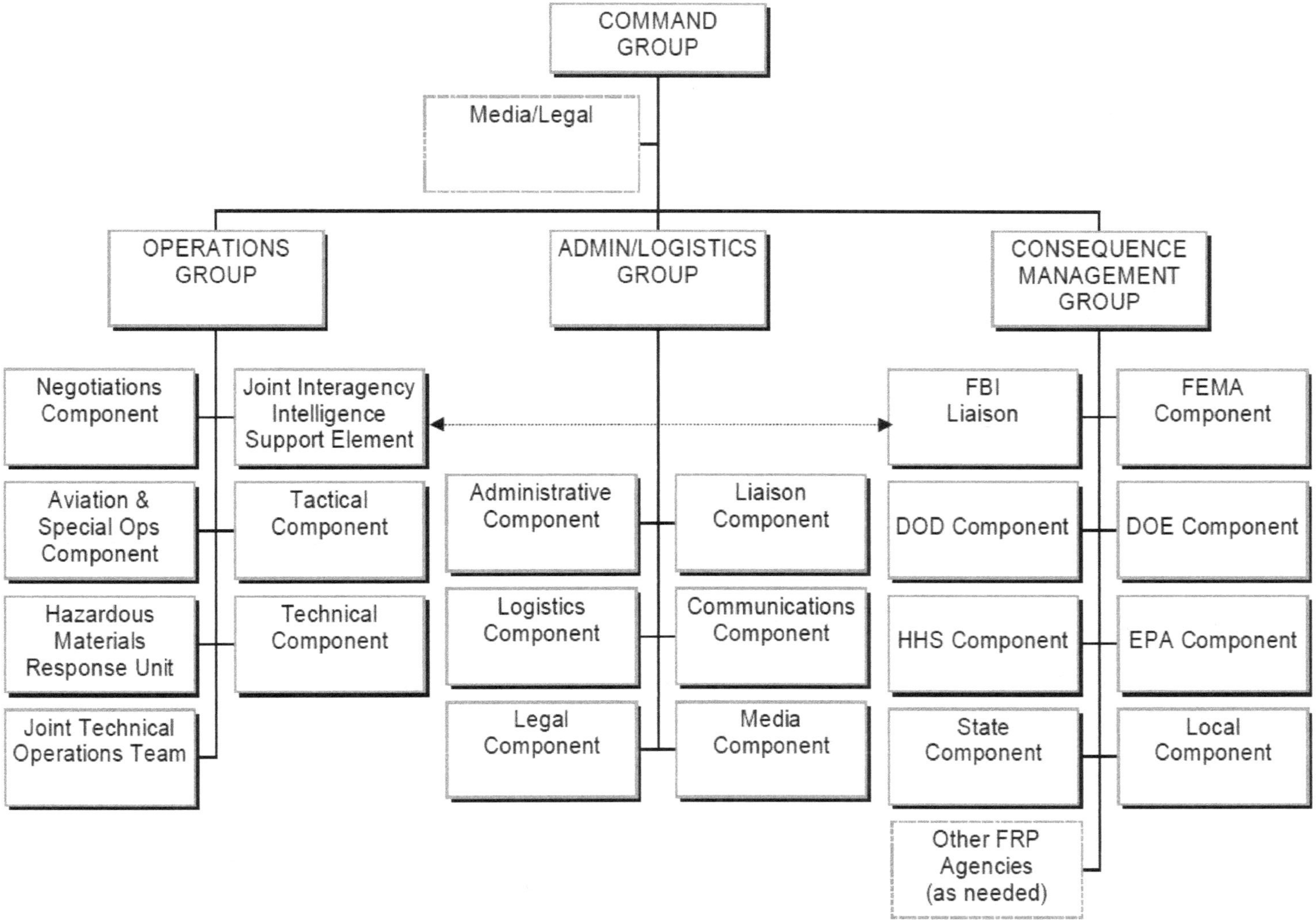

Figure 4 - Joint Operations Center

COMMAND GROUP

Media/Legal

OPERATIONS GROUP

- Negotiations Component
- Aviation & Special Ops Component
- Hazardous Materials Response Unit
- Joint Technical Operations Team
- Joint Interagency Intelligence Support Element
- Tactical Component
- Technical Component

ADMIN/LOGISTICS GROUP

- Administrative Component
- Logistics Component
- Legal Component
- Liaison Component
- Communications Component
- Media Component

CONSEQUENCE MANAGEMENT GROUP

- FBI Liaison
- DOD Component
- HHS Component
- State Component
- Other FRP Agencies (as needed)
- FEMA Component
- DOE Component
- EPA Component
- Local Component

A FEMA representative coordinates the actions of the JOC Consequence Management Group, and expedites activation of a Federal consequence management response should it become necessary. FBI and FEMA representatives will screen threat/incident intelligence for the Consequence Management Group. The JOC Consequence Management Group monitors the crisis management response in order to advise on decisions that may have implications for consequence management, and to provide continuity should a Federal consequence management response become necessary.

Should the threat of a terrorist incident become imminent, the JOC Consequence Management Group may forward recommendations to the ROC Director to initiate limited pre-deployment of assets under the Stafford Act. Authority to make decisions regarding FRP operations rests with the ROC Director until an FCO is appointed. The senior FEMA official in the JOC ensures appropriate coordination between FRP operations and the JOC Command Group.

4. On-Scene Coordination

Once a WMD incident has occurred (with or without a pre-release crisis period), local government emergency response organizations will respond to the incident scene and appropriate notifications to local, State, and Federal authorities will be made. Control of this incident scene will be established by local response authorities (likely a senior fire or law enforcement official). Command and control of the incident scene is vested with the Incident Commander/Unified Command. Operational control of assets at the scene is retained by the designated officials representing the agency (local, State, or Federal) providing the assets. These officials manage tactical operations at the scene in coordination with the UC as directed by their agency counterparts at field-level operational centers, if used. As mutual aid partners, State and Federal responders arrive to augment the local responders. The incident command structure that was initially established will likely transition into a Unified Command (UC). This UC structure will facilitate both crisis and consequence management activities. The UC structure used at the scene will expand as support units and agency representatives arrive to support crisis and consequence management operations. On-scene consequence management activities will be supported by the local and State EOC, which will be augmented by the ROC or Disaster Field Office, and the Emergency Support Team, as appropriate.

When Federal resources arrive at the scene, they will operate as a Forward Coordinating Team (FCT). The senior FBI representative will join the Unified Command group while the senior FEMA representative will coordinate activity of Federal consequence management liaisons to the Unified Command. On-scene Federal crisis management resources will be organized into a separate FBI Crisis Management Branch within the Operations Section, and an FBI representative will serve as Deputy to the Operations Section Chief. Federal consequence management resources will assist the appropriate ICS function, as directed (see Figure 5).

Throughout the incident, the actions and activities of the Unified Command at the incident scene and the Command Group of the JOC will be continuously and completely coordinated.

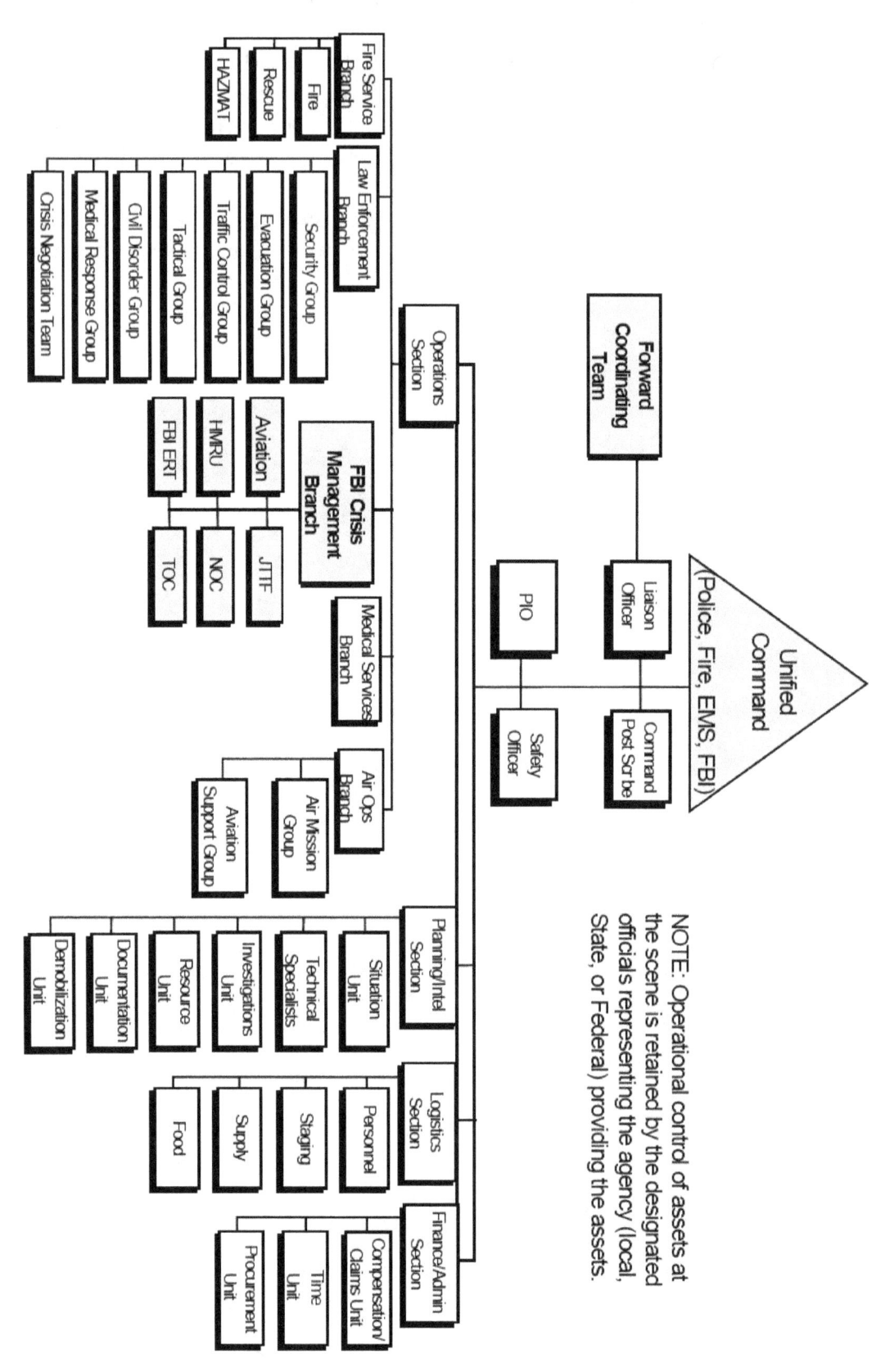

Figure 5 – On-Scene Coordination

NOTE: Operational control of assets at the scene is retained by the designated agency (local, State, or Federal) providing the assets.

V.   PHASING OF THE FEDERAL RESPONSE

Phasing of the Federal response to a threat or act of terrorism includes Notification; Activation and Deployment; Response Operations; Response Deactivation; and Recovery. Phases may be abbreviated or bypassed when warranted.

A.   Notification

Receipt of a terrorist threat or incident may be through any source or medium, may be articulated, or developed through intelligence sources. It is the responsibility of all local, State, and Federal agencies and departments to notify the FBI when such a threat is received.

Upon receipt of a threat of domestic terrorism, the FBI will conduct a formal threat credibility assessment of the information with assistance from select interagency experts. For a WMD threat, this includes three perspectives:

- Technical feasibility: An assessment of the capacity of the threatening individual or organization to obtain or produce the material at issue;

- Operational practicability: An assessment of the feasibility of delivering or employing the material in the manner threatened;

- Behavioral resolve: A psychological assessment of the likelihood that the subject(s) will carry out the threat, including a review of any written or verbal statement by the subject(s).

The FBI manages a Terrorist Threat Warning System to ensure that vital information regarding terrorism reaches those in the U.S. counterterrorism and law enforcement community responsible for countering terrorist threats. This information is transmitted via secure teletype. Each message transmitted under this system is an alert, an advisory, or an assessment—an alert if the terrorist threat is credible and specific; an advisory if the threat is credible but general in both timing and target; or an assessment to impart facts and/or threat analysis concerning terrorism.

1.   The role of the FBI is to:

a.   Verify the accuracy of the notification,

b.   Initiate the threat assessment process,

c.   Notify Domestic Emergency Support Team agencies, and

     d.   Notify other Federal, State and local agencies, as appropriate.

    2.   **The role of FEMA is to:**

     a.   Advise the FBI of consequence management considerations,

     b.   Verify that the State and local governments have been notified, and

     c.   Notify other Federal agencies under the FRP, as appropriate.

B.   **Activation and Deployment**

Upon determination that the threat is credible, or an act of terrorism has occurred, FBIHQ will initiate appropriate liaison with other Federal agencies to activate their operations centers and provide liaison officers to the SIOC. In addition, FBIHQ will initiate communications with the SAC of the responsible Field Office apprising him/her of possible courses of action and discussing deployment of the DEST. The FBI SAC will establish initial operational priorities based upon the specific circumstances of the threat or incident. This information will then be forwarded to FBIHQ to coordinate identification and deployment of appropriate resources.

Based upon a credible threat assessment and a request by the SAC, the FBI Director, in consultation with the Attorney General, may request authorization through National Security Council groups to deploy the DEST to assist the SAC in mitigating the crisis situation. The DEST is a rapidly deployable, inter-agency team responsible for providing the FBI expert advice and support concerning the U.S. Government's capabilities in resolving the terrorist threat or incident. This includes crisis and consequence management assistance, technical or scientific advice and contingency planning guidance tailored to situations involving chemical, biological, or nuclear/radiological weapons.

Upon arrival at the FBI Command Post or forward location, the DEST may act as a stand alone advisory team to the SAC providing recommended courses of action. While the DEST can operate as an advance element of the JOC, DEST deployment does not have to precede JOC activation. Upon JOC activation, the SAC is the Federal On-Scene Commander (OSC). The Federal OSC serves as the on-scene manager for the United States Government and coordinates the actions of the JOC Command Group. The DEST consequence management component merges into the JOC structure under the leadership of the Senior FEMA Official.

1. **The role of the FBI is to:**

   a.   Designate a Federal OSC,

   b.   Deploy the DEST if warranted and approved, and provide liaison to State and local authorities as appropriate,

   c.   Establish multi-agency coordination structures, as appropriate, at the incident scene, area, and national level in order to:

   > (1)   Coordinate the determination of operational objectives, strategies, and priorities for the use of critical resources that have been allocated to the situation, and communicate multi-agency decisions back to individual agencies and incidents.

   > (2)   Coordinate the evaluation of emerging incidents, prioritization of incidents, and projection of future needs.

   > (3)   Establish a Joint Information Center and coordinate information dissemination.

2. **The role of FEMA is to:**

   a.   Activate the appropriate FRP elements, as needed,

   b.   Designate and deploy an individual to serve as the Senior FEMA Official to the JOC. Primary responsibilities include:

   > (1)   Managing the Consequence Management Group.

   > (2)   Serving as senior consequence management official on the Command Group.

   > (3)   Designate an individual to work with the FBI liaison to screen intelligence for consequence management related implications.

   c.   Identify the appropriate agencies to staff the JOC Consequence Management Group and advise the FBI. With FBI concurrence, notify consequence management agencies to request they deploy representatives to the JOC.

C.   Response Operations

The response operations phase involves those activities necessary for an actual Federal response to address the immediate and short-term effects of a terrorist threat or incident. These activities support an emergency response with a bilateral focus on the achievement of law enforcement goals and objectives, and the planning and execution of consequence management activities to address the effects of a terrorist incident. Prior to the use or functioning of a WMD, crisis management activities will generally have priority. When an incident results in the use of WMD, consequence management activities will generally have priority. Activities may overlap and/or run concurrently during the emergency response, and are dependent on the threat and/or the strategies for responding to the incident. Events may preclude certain activities from occurring, particularly in an attack without prior warning.

D.   Response Deactivation

Each Federal agency will discontinue emergency response operations under the CONPLAN when advised that their assistance is no longer required in support of the FBI, or when their statutory responsibilities have been fulfilled.

Upon determination that applicable law enforcement goals and objectives have been met, no further immediate threat exists, and that Federal crisis management actions are no longer required, the Attorney General, in consultation with the FBI Director and the FEMA Director, shall transfer the LFA role to FEMA. The Federal OSC will deactivate and discontinue emergency response operations under the CONPLAN. Prior to this activity, the Federal OSC will apprise the senior officials representing agencies in the JOC Command Group of the intent to deactivate in order to confirm agreement for this decision.

Consequence management support to the State and local government(s) impacted by the incident may continue for a very long period. Termination of consequence management assistance will be handled according to the procedures established in the FRP.

E.   Recovery

The State and local governments share primary responsibility for planning the recovery of the affected area. Recovery efforts will be initiated at the request of the State or local governments following mutual agreement of the agencies involved and confirmation from the LFA that the incident has stabilized and that no further threat exists to public health and safety. The Federal government will assist the State and local governments in developing mitigation and recovery plans, with FEMA coordinating the overall activity of the Federal agencies involved in this phase.

APPENDIX A: ACRONYMS

CONPLAN	Concept of Operations Plan
DEST	Domestic Emergency Support Team
DOD	Department of Defense
DOE	Department of Energy
DOJ	Department of Justice
EM	Emergency Management
EMS	Emergency Medical Services
EOC	Emergency Operations Center
EPA	Environmental Protection Agency
ERT	Evidence Response Team (FBI)
FBI	Federal Bureau of Investigation
FCO	Federal Coordinating Officer
FEMA	Federal Emergency Management Agency
FRP	Federal Response Plan
HAZMAT	Hazardous Materials
HHS	Department of Health and Human Services
HMRU	Hazardous Materials Response Unit
JIC	Joint Information Center
JIISE	Joint Interagency Intelligence Support Element
JOC	Joint Operations Center
JTTF	Joint Terrorism Task Force
ICS	Incident Command System
LFA	Lead Federal Agency
NCP	National Oil and Hazardous Substances Pollution Contingency Plan
NOC	Negotiations Operations Center
OSC	On-Scene Commander (FBI)
	On-Scene Coordinator (EPA)
PIO	Public Information Officer
PDD-39	Presidential Decision Directive 39
ROC	Regional Operations Center
SAC	Special Agent-in-Charge
SFO	Senior FEMA Official
SIOC	Strategic Information and Operations Center
STOC	Sniper Tactical Operations Center
TOC	Tactical Operations Center
UC	Unified Command
USCG	United States Coast Guard
WMD	Weapon of Mass Destruction

APPENDIX B: DEFINITIONS

Assessment - The evaluation and interpretation of measurements and other information to provide a basis for decision-making.

Combating Terrorism - The full range of Federal programs and activities applied against terrorism, domestically and abroad, regardless of the source or motive.

Consequence Management - Consequence management is predominantly an emergency management function and includes measures to protect public health and safety, restore essential government services, and provide emergency relief to governments, businesses, and individuals affected by the consequences of terrorism. In an actual or potential terrorist incident, a consequence management response will be managed by FEMA using structures and resources of the Federal Response Plan (FRP). These efforts will include support missions as described in other Federal operations plans, such as predictive modeling, protective action recommendations, and mass decontamination.

Coordinate - To advance systematically an exchange of information among principals who have or may have a need to know certain information in order to carry out their role in a response.

Counterterrorism - The full range of activities directed against terrorism, including preventive, deterrent, response and crisis management efforts.

Crisis Management - Crisis management is predominantly a law enforcement function and includes measures to identify, acquire, and plan the use of resources needed to anticipate, prevent, and/or resolve a threat or act of terrorism. In a terrorist incident, a crisis management response may include traditional law enforcement missions, such as intelligence, surveillance, tactical operations, negotiations, forensics, and investigations, as well as technical support missions, such as agent identification, search, render safe procedures, transfer and disposal, and limited decontamination. In addition to the traditional law enforcement missions, crisis management also includes assurance of public health and safety.

Disaster Field Office (DFO) - The office established in or near the designated area to support Federal and State response and recovery operations. The Disaster Field Office houses the Federal Coordinating Officer (FCO), the Emergency Response Team, and, where possible, the State Coordinating Officer and support Staff.

Emergency - Any natural or man-caused situation that results in or may result in substantial injury or harm to the population or substantial damage to or loss of property.

Emergency Operations Center (EOC)- The site from which civil government officials (municipal, county, State and Federal) exercise direction and control in an emergency.

Emergency Public Information - Information which is disseminated primarily in anticipation of an emergency or at the actual time of an emergency and in addition to providing information, frequently directs actions, instructs, and transmits direct orders.

Emergency Response Team - (1) A team composed of Federal program and support personnel, which FEMA activates and deploys into an area affected by a major disaster or emergency. This team assists the FCO in carrying out his/her responsibilities under the Stafford Act, the declaration, applicable laws, regulations, and the FEMA-State agreement. (2) The team is an interagency team, consisting of the lead representative from each Federal department or agency assigned primary responsibility for an Emergency support Function and key members of the FCO's staff, formed to assist the FCO in carrying out his/her responsibilities. The team provides a forum for coordinating the overall Federal consequence management response requirements.

Emergency Support Function - A functional area of response activity established to facilitate coordinated Federal delivery of assistance required during the response phase to save lives, protect property and health, and maintain public safety. These functions represent those types of Federal assistance which the State likely will need most because of the overwhelming impact of a catastrophic event on local and State resources.

Evacuation - Organized, phased, and supervised dispersal of civilians from dangerous or potentially dangerous areas, and their reception and care in safe areas.

Federal Coordinating Officer (FCO) - (1) The person appointed by the FEMA Director, or in his/her absence, the FEMA Deputy Director, or alternatively the FEMA Associate Director for Response and Recovery, following a declaration of a major disaster or of an emergency by the President, to coordinate Federal assistance. The FCO initiates action immediately to assure that Federal Assistance is provided in accordance with the declaration, applicable laws, regulations, and the FEMA-State agreement. (2) The FCO is the senior Federal official appointed in accordance with the provisions of Public Law 93-288, as amended (the Stafford Act), to coordinate the overall consequence management response and recovery activities. The FCO represents the President as provided by Section 303 of the Stafford Act for the purpose of coordinating the administration of Federal relief activities in the designated area. Additionally, the FCO is delegated responsibilities and performs those for the FEMA Director as outlined in Executive Order 12148 and those responsibilities delegated to the FEMA Regional Director in the Code of Federal Regulations, Title 44, Part 205.

Federal On-Scene Commander (OSC) - The FBI official designated upon JOC activation to ensure appropriate coordination of the overall United States government response with Federal, State and local authorities, until such time as the Attorney General transfers the LFA role to FEMA.

Federal Response Plan (FRP) - (1) The plan designed to address the consequences of any disaster or emergency situation in which there is a need for Federal assistance under the authorities of the Robert T. Stafford Disaster Relief and Emergency Assistance Act, 42 U. S.C. 5 121 et seq. (2) The FRP is the Federal government's plan of action for assisting affected States and local jurisdictions in the event of a major disaster or emergency.

First Responder - Local police, fire, and emergency medical personnel who first arrive on the scene of an incident and take action to save lives, protect property, and meet basic human needs.

Joint Information Center (JIC) - A center established to coordinate the Federal public information activities on-scene. It is the central point of contact for all news media at the scene of the incident. Public information officials from all participating Federal agencies should collocate at the JIC. Public information officials from participating State and local agencies also may collocate at the JIC.

Joint Interagency Intelligence Support Element (JIISE) - The JIISE is an interagency intelligence component designed to fuse intelligence information from the various agencies participating in a response to a WMD threat or incident within an FBI JOC. The JIISE is an expanded version of the investigative/intelligence component which is part of the standardized FBI command post structure. The JIISE manages five functions including: security, collections management, current intelligence, exploitation, and dissemination.

Joint Operations Center (JOC) - Established by the LFA under the operational control of the Federal OSC, as the focal point for management and direction of onsite activities, coordination/establishment of State requirements/priorities, and coordination of the overall Federal response.

Lead Agency - The Federal department or agency assigned lead responsibility under U.S. law to manage and coordinate the Federal response in a specific functional area. For the purposes of the CONPLAN, there are two lead agencies, the FBI for Crisis Management and FEMA for Consequence Management. Lead agencies support the overall Lead Federal Agency (LFA) during all phases of the response.

Lead Federal Agency (LFA) - The agency designated by the President to lead and coordinate the overall Federal response is referred to as the LFA and is determined by the type of emergency. In general, an LFA establishes operational structures and procedures to assemble and work with agencies providing direct support to the LFA in order to provide an initial assessment of the situation; develop an action plan; monitor and update operational priorities; and ensure each agency exercises its concurrent and distinct authorities under US law and supports the LFA in carrying out the President's relevant policy. Specific responsibilities of an LFA vary according to the agency's unique statutory authorities.

Liaison - An agency official sent to another agency to facilitate interagency communications and coordination.

Local Government - Any county, city, village, town, district, or political subdivision of any State, and Indian tribe or authorized tribal organization, or Alaska Native village or organization, including any rural community or unincorporated town or village or any other public entity.

On-Scene Coordinator (OSC) - The Federal official pre-designated by the EPA and U.S. Coast Guard to coordinate and direct response and removals under the National Oil and Hazardous Substances Pollution Contingency Plan.

Public Information Officer - Official at headquarters or in the field responsible for preparing and coordinating the dissemination of public information in cooperation with other responding Federal, State, and local agencies.

Recovery - Recovery, in this document, includes all types of emergency actions dedicated to the continued protection of the public or to promoting the resumption of normal activities in the affected area.

Recovery Plan - A plan developed by each State, with assistance from the responding Federal agencies, to restore the affected area.

Regional Director - The Director of one of FEMA's ten regional offices and principal representative for working with other Federal regions, State and local governments, and the private sector in that jurisdiction.

Regional Operations Center (ROC) - The temporary operations facility for the coordination of Federal response and recovery activities, located at the FEMA Regional Office (or at the Federal Regional Center) and led by the FEMA Regional Director or Deputy Regional Director until the Disaster Field Office becomes operational.

Response - Those activities and programs designed to address the immediate and short-term effects of the onset of an emergency or disaster.

Senior FEMA Official (SFO) - The official appointed by the Director of FEMA, or his representative, that is responsible for deploying to the JOC to: (1) serve as the senior interagency consequence management representative on the Command Group, and (2) manage and coordinate activities taken by the Consequence Management Group.

State Coordinating Officer - An official designated by the Governor of the affected State, upon a declaration of a major disaster or emergency, to coordinate State and local disaster assistance efforts with those of the Federal government, and to act in cooperation with the FCO to administer disaster recovery efforts.

Terrorism - Terrorism includes the unlawful use of force or violence against persons or property to intimidate or coerce a government, the civilian population, or any segment thereof, in furtherance of political or social objectives.

Weapon of Mass Destruction (WMD) - A WMD is any device, material, or substance used in a manner, in a quantity or type, or under circumstances evidencing an intent to cause death or serious injury to persons or significant damage to property.

www.ingramcontent.com/pod-product-compliance
Lightning Source LLC
Chambersburg PA
CBHW081759280526
45789CB00008B/2924